Rescued From The Jaws Of Death
Encapsulate of victory

Bolaji L Adebiyi

WESTBOW
PRESS®
A DIVISION OF THOMAS NELSON
& ZONDERVAN

Copyright © 2019 Bolaji L Adebiyi.

All rights reserved. No part of this book may be used or reproduced by any means, graphic, electronic, or mechanical, including photocopying, recording, taping or by any information storage retrieval system without the written permission of the author except in the case of brief quotations embodied in critical articles and reviews.

WestBow Press books may be ordered through booksellers or by contacting:

WestBow Press
A Division of Thomas Nelson & Zondervan
1663 Liberty Drive
Bloomington, IN 47403
www.westbowpress.com
1 (866) 928-1240

Because of the dynamic nature of the Internet, any web addresses or links contained in this book may have changed since publication and may no longer be valid. The views expressed in this work are solely those of the author and do not necessarily reflect the views of the publisher, and the publisher hereby disclaims any responsibility for them.

Any people depicted in stock imagery provided by Getty Images are models, and such images are being used for illustrative purposes only. Certain stock imagery © Getty Images.

All Scripture quotations, unless otherwise indicated, are taken from the Holy Bible, New International Version®, NIV®. Copyright ©1973, 1978, 1984, 2011 by Biblica, Inc.™ Used by permission of Zondervan. All rights reserved worldwide. www.zondervan.com The "NIV" and "New International Version" are trademarks registered in the United States Patent and Trademark Office by Biblica, Inc.™

Scripture taken from the King James Version of the Bible.

ISBN: 978-1-9736-6808-4 (sc)
ISBN: 978-1-9736-6807-7 (e)

Print information available on the last page.

WestBow Press rev. date: 7/17/2019

Table of Contents

Appreciation vii

Author's Profile xi

Dedication xiii

Introduction xv

Chapter 1 Background Information 1

Chapter 2 How It All Began 2

            First hospital experience 2

Chapter 3 My Experience At Rehab 17

Chapter 4 Divine Encounter 29

Chapter 5 Prophecy Fulfilled-The New Life 48

            The Things that I have Learned on this
            Journey 50

Conclusion 57

Epilogue 63

Appreciation

I am grateful to my God, my saviour Jesus Christ and the Holy Spirit for the encounter and opportunity that I had with GOD overtime. Without the inspiration of the Holy Spirit and the protection of Jesus Christ, this book would have been impossible. I would have been lost or passed to the great beyond if not for God, Jesus Christ and the Holy Spirit.

I appreciate my saviour Jesus Christ for shedding his blood on the Cross to redeem my life and soul from the devil by making an open show of the devil by triumphing over him.

Colossians 2:14-15 *Blotting out the handwriting of ordinances that was against us, which was contrary to us, and took it out of the way, nailing it to his cross; And having spoiled principalities and powers, he made a shew of them openly, triumphing over them in it.*

I am grateful to God for giving me another chance, a second chance and an opportunity to love Him, to serve Him, to use my story to win souls for Christ. Also, I thank God for using my testimony to encourage those that are in Christ to evangelize God's mercy and grace to all and sundry.

Moreover, I appreciate Jesus for granting me a special opportunity to fulfil my purpose in life.

According to Psalm 57:2 *I will cry unto God Most High, unto God that performeth all things for me.*

I thank and honour my husband, Olabanji Bartholomew Adebiyi and my children, Joyce, Peace and Gracious, for standing by me throughout the time of the illness. I simply cannot ask or wish for something more. Thank you all for your perseverance and untiring support during my hospitalisation. I often marvel how God blessed me with all of them; also, I always thank God whenever I reflect on how much we have all grown to trust Jesus and build confidence in the power of faith and prayer.

I express gratitude to Daddy Adebiyi (popularly called ba-eleja) and mummy(iya Lekiti) for their daily prayers. Respect and love for the for the entire Idowu family for their kind support and prayers.I wish that my late parents, Gabriel Adekola Idowu and Susanna Jumoke Idowu were alive to see the woman that I have become since Jesus took over my life. May their souls rest in eternal peace.

I appreciate Ayodele Idowu (UK) and every of my brothers and sisters that God used to raise me up since I was a child. I love the manifestation of the Lord Jesus in you. I thank evangelist Adekola Idowu, Pastor Adetutu Morolari and my brothers and sisters for taking good care of me and trusting God for my recovery when I was on the bed of affliction. Thank you Idowu Adedare and Idowu banjo. And Particularly my sisters and brothers who send me prayers.

I thank my brother-in-law, Yomi Adebiyi (UK) and Ayodeji Adebiyi (USA), including Mrs Bunmi Adebiyi (USA) for their visits and relentless prayers. And all my brother and sisters in my Adebiyi family.

My deepest gratitude to Pastors Tunde and Bukola Babalola my spiritual parents in the Lord, at RCCG All Saints Parish, Portlaoise, Ireland including every member of the parish, They were unwavering in their support and prayers. They constantly built my faith and assuring me that everything would be alright. Well, glory be to God everything is all right now!

Moreover, I express my heartfelt thanks to my god-parents, Major General (Pastor) Ade Adefolalu (rtd) and Mrs Grace Adefolalu for always reminding me of my purpose in life and for standing by me in prayers during my tough times in the hospital. Among many friends and well-wishers, just too numerous for me to mention I want to appreciate the families of Mr & mrs Wole Idowu, Mr & mrs Ayodele, Mr & mrs Emmanuel, Mr&mrsAdeshiyan, Mr & mrs Oladapo and sister Faith. I express my sincere gratitude to all friends that came to bathe me in the hospital, those who daily brought hot meals for me, and those who sent regular messages and held prayer sessions frequently for my recovery.

I am short of the right words to adequately express my invaluable appreciation to the entire staff of Naas Hospital and the Mater Hospital Dublin, particularly staff of the Coronary Care Unit (CCU), who really took good care of me. The memories of your loving care linger in my mind. I also received highly specialised care from Midland Regional Portlaoise Hospital; I am grateful to all staff that took care of me there. I appreciate the support of the staff of the National Rehabilitation Hospital, Dun-Laoghaire, Dublin.

I thank all messengers of God and brethren in Christ in different parts of the world, particular my families and friends in Ireland, Nigeria, the UK and the US too numerous to mention, who spent days and months in prayer, fasting and placing a demand on God's mercy for my recovery. Thank you pastor Mathew Omotoso. I express my gratitude to Mr Olusanmi Amujo, for providing advice and editorial support to me while writing this book. I thank Ms Bola Praise for encouraging me to write the book.

I thank those who are praying for me as they read this book; the mercy of God will never depart from you and your entire household in the mighty name of Jesus.

I thank Mr. Bola Praise for encouraging me to write the book, I appreciate Seyi Bamisaye(uk) you are more than a friend.

Author's Profile

Bolaji Adebiyi is a woman with a humorous, youthful heart and a burning passion to share her miraculous story of God's healing power with the entire world.

Bolaji grew up in Nigeria where she became a fully qualified accountant.

She has lived in the Republic of Ireland for over a decade and worked as a Social Care Worker after qualifying with an honours degree in Applied Social Studies. Presently, she does voluntary work with the teenagers and young adults.

While in Nigeria, she attended the Word of Faith Bible Institute at Winners Chapel, Lagos, Nigeria. She further attended the Redeemer Bible College in Ireland.

Bolaji is a lover of Jesus Christ and she goes to places where the Holy Spirit leads her to share the testimonyof her deliverance with brethren.She has shared the testimony of God's awesome deliverance of her life from the jaws of death with thousands of people and God has shown up in the lives of many who believed in the healing power of Jesus Christ in those places. She wants the world to hear about the miraculous power of Jesus Christ and believe that miracles do happen on a daily basis. She desires to encourage and enhance the faith of believers that what the Lord did for her, He can do for all, including the person reading this book.

Dedication

If it had not been the Lord who was on my side, I would not have been here today to write this book. I am giving all the glory to my Saviour and my Redeemer, Jesus Christ called *Agbanilagbatan* in my Nigerian native language meaning the God that delivers completely.

I cannot overemphasize how grateful and thankful I am to Jesus Christ the lover of my soul for dying on that Cross and rescuing me with his precious blood. I never knew that Jesus could favour me this way; Lord, who am I that you think of me?

I dedicate this book to my children, Joyce, Peace and Gracious Adebiyi for their indescribable love towards me before, during and after the hospital experience. I commend their fearlessness in the face of my spiritual battle; they were praying daily for me, encouraging me and confidently assuring me while I was bed bound in hospital that I was coming home soon, despite the fact that they didn't know when or how I would return home. May God bless you all for standing by me to fight the battle of my survival together.

Introduction

The summary of the testimonies I am about to share in this book can be found in Psalm 124:1-7:

> *¹If it had not been the LORD who was on our side, now may Israel say;*
>
> *²If it had not been the LORD who was on our side, when men rose up against us:*
>
> *³Then they had swallowed us up quick, when their wrath was kindled against us:*
>
> *⁴Then the waters had overwhelmed us, the stream had gone over our soul:*
>
> *⁵Then the proud waters had gone over our soul.*
>
> *⁶Blessed be the LORD, who hath not given us as a prey to their teeth.*

7Our soul is escaped as a bird out of the snare of the fowlers: the snare is broken, and we are escaped.

The journey of twenty one month hospitalisation and the indescribable pains that I experienced daily, coupled with the deliverance from death that followed, have made me realise and believe that God has a purpose for my life. The divine opportunity to survive the ravaging jaws of death brings me closer to fulfilling the purpose for which God rescued me to accomplish in life.

Esther 4:14*For if thou altogether holdest thy peace at this time, then shall there enlargement and deliverance arise to the Jews from another place; but thou and thy father's house shall be destroyed: and who knoweth whether thou art come to the kingdom for such a time as this?*

Rick Warren described purpose as "nothing matters more than knowing God's purpose for your life and that nothing can compensate for not knowing."

If not for making it possible by Jesus for me to discover or understand my purpose in life, it would have been impossible to write this book. Once you know your purpose in life and follow it, then you are truly living. I personally did not realize that God could use me as a living testimony of what He can do for His children. I never thought that He would use my story to bless and encourage others. Of course, I love God and all that He represents in the Bible and the world. But, I was equally contented with gaining employment and building a career to support my family and give to charity. However, I never bothered until now to openly proclaim Jesus as a healer and deliverer. Prior to the sickness, I didn't know that Jesus could favour and use me in a way to publicise His healing powers to mankind. I was contented with just being a channel of receiving God's blessing. It did not occur to me that Jesus intended to use my testimony as source of rescue to the body of Christ. It is an honour and a divine privilege that I do not take for granted at all.

Praise God for His unending supply of our needs. It is disturbing that a lot of Church people, including my self just want to receive from God like little babies; we often want to take more from God all the time because He is *Jehovah-Jireh* (God my provider). some Christians do not realise that God has created us to be givers to others; one of the purposes for which He created us is to be a channel of giving to other people. God wants to love the world through us. I am praying today for a reader of this book that you will find fulfilmentof destiny in your life before you go to meet your Lord in the mighty name of Jesus.

I believe God that my story will give you hope and encouragement that no matter what you are going through right now, it is not over with you until God says it is over. I challenge you with this book not to give up on yourself because Jesus has not given up on you. God specialises in doing things that are impossible with mere men. He is a loving Father and He allows us to go through stuff for us to be vessels of honour for His use. The Bible declared in Romans 5:3-5:

> *³And not only so, but we glory in tribulations also: knowing that tribulation worketh patience;*
>
> *⁴And patience, experience; and experience, hope:*
>
> *⁵And hope maketh not ashamed; because the love of God is shed abroad in our hearts by the Holy Ghost which is given unto us.*

I wouldn't have understood the kind of pain that those in the hospital go through if I had not gone through the storm of sickness. Up until now, I cannot describe the pain I went through, but I can easily relate to what it means to be in a helpless and hopeless situation on the hospital bed because I was in a prolonged sickness too. Which is why I can say to you, I get it! I understand it! I feel it! I experience it!

If there are brethren going through affliction of any kind, I am encouraging you not to give up; don't waste all that pain, use it by channelling it to proclaim the love, grace and mercy of our Lord Jesus Christ to the whole world. I pray that every kind of pain that you are going through, I see the power of the Holy Spirit come upon you by faith and set you free this hour in the name of the Lord Jesus Christ.

1

Background Information

My very first encounter with the Lord was when I was about twelve years old; during this period I came across a book with the story of the death of Jesus Christ on the Cross. The pictures in the book were in colour; the marks and cuts on the body of Jesus, including the nails that went through His hands and legs, were vividly shown and they cut deep into my heart.

As a child, I held on to the book many days and nights; I cried at what Jesus must have gone through. I felt so much compassion for Him and I vowed in my little mind then to avenge the persons that treated Him that way. Not knowing that I was the one that made Jesus Christ experienced the pains that He went through on His way to Calvary and on the Cross.

2

How It All Began

First hospital experience

I woke up in the evening in the hospital beautifully dressed in makeup, eyelashes and foundation. I remembered the doctors asking the nurses if my foundation was a drop of blood as it had stained the hospital's white sheets. I later discovered they had fixed something like a cast into my two legs to keep them from twisting. Thereafter, the doctor came to inform me that I had suffered a stroke. It was a devastating news I least expected .After the stroke, I woke up in the hospital, and it later dawned on me that it was going to take at least twelve months or even more to fully recover from the stroke.

With my professional background and experience in working in the healthcare sector with people experiencing disabilities, I knew the ramification of the health and physical challenges involved in managing stroke. The fear of the consequences of stroke gripped my mind for a moment. I could not come to terms with the fact that it happened to me. Without any doubt in my mind, I possess the basic knowledge and understanding about the risk factors and causes of stroke such as high blood pressure, cigarette smoking, diabetes, poor diet, excess body weight and obesity, physical inactivity, high blood cholesterol, family history of stroke, carotid artery disease, peripheral artery disease, coronary heart disease, sickle cell disease and bad brain health among others.

A multitude of thoughts raced through my mind as I was trying to identify where I was culpable of any lapses. While fighting the hard reality of having a stroke in my mind, I realised my helplessness as I knew that treating stroke could be a long haul. I came into a blunt conclusion that only the Great Physician, Jesus Christ could help me as I had exhausted my personal abilities to fight back.

In spite the daunting problems associated with stroke, I tried hard to ignite my faith by preventing fear from overwhelming my trust in God. No matter the intensity of adversity confronting a believer in Jesus Christ, faith will always overcome fear. Fear always compounds the problems associated with a spiritual challenge and makes every situation more difficult to deal with.

Dealing with a chronic illness or a terminal disease when we believe that Jesus Christ heals is a fight that many Christians do not want to undertake. As human beings, we want a microwave-like recovery after illness, but some Christians that had undergone prolonged sickness might tell you that there were times they thought God, Jesus Christ and Holy Spirit were silent when they called them to intervene in their recovery. There are times I also thought Heaven was silent, but I believe when Jesus Christ is silent He is working out my miracle.

Bolaji L Adebiyi

It is important to understand the nature of our Lord Jesus Christ while He was on earth; we should bring the understanding to bear on our healing expectations during our prayers for recovery. Honestly, I know it is not easy for a Christian to wait for a long time in expectation of divine intervention when passing through agonising affliction on the hospital bed .Having experienced life-threatening and harrowing affliction, I understand why we often want an instantaneous answer when we call Jesus Christ to heal us. I experienced a similar situation on many occasions that I wanted Jesus Christ to act immediately. But, in my quiet moments, I often reflected on the nature of our Lord, who was not a noisemaker when He was on earth, to get some consolation. I learned that Jesus is not moved by our anxiety, noisemaking, fretting and complaining, He is moved by our strong faith, trust and reliance on Him when everything looks gloomy and hopeless to mankind. He does His mighty acts gently and quietly; up until today, He still remains the gentle Lamb of God. When we call during the time of affliction and Heaven remains silent the Word of the Lord in 1 Kings 19:11-13 should give us a consolation not to despair.

My experience in the hospital was better described as traumatic, not because I did not get the best treatment; the truth is I was provided with the best medical treatment and support available. Besides, my pastors, other ministers of the gospel and brethren did not relent in providing spiritual support to complement medical treatment. They stood in the gap praying, fasting and giving thanks to God in expectation of His miraculous in my life. The reason behind my upsetting experience in the hospital was the sudden awareness that I used to be a very active person only few days ago; I could do what I wanted to do physically; I

4

Rescued From The Claws Of Death

could walk, run, drive a car and engage in conversations effortlessly, but suddenly all those activities were terminated like a flash of lightning.

My powerlessness and the rude shock of my immobility due to confinement on the hospital bed led to internal revulsion. I was angry about my bedridden condition; I was furious with myself that given my knowledge of healthcare, I didn't see it coming at all. I hated my situation on the hospital bed and it pained me that I could not change the situation at will. For about one week, I was not allowed to get up or sit up; it was extremely disturbing for the first time that I had to use the bedpans to pass waste from my system.

I personally love independence to do things on my own without being at the mercy of anyone or being a burden to my husband and children. I am particular about the way i look as much as posssible; Brethren, the thoughts that I couldn't do any of these tasks, including my inability to go to the workplace as well as attend my postgraduate programme, were highly depressing. The idea that I suddenly became dependent on other people made me extremely uncomfortable and unhappy. I came to a vexing understanding of the emptiness of boast, exaggeration and pride of human beings which we often utter without a sense of humility; I came to realise the emptiness of boastful statements such as "I have control over my affairs" or "I am in control of my life or I can do and undo". Now I discovered that no man or woman is in control of his or her life in the absence of good health. As if a sudden flash of lightning lit everything up in my mind for a second, I understood the huge import of "health is wealth". In my distressing situation, I hung steadfastly to the truth of the Word of God that

When you pass through the waters, I will be with you and when you pass through the rivers, they will not sweep over you. When you walk

Bolaji L Adebiyi

through the fire, you will not be burned; the flames will not set you ablaze. (Isaiah 43:2, NIV).

Despite the relief that I had when I remembered the scripture above, the first thing that came to mind was denial. I was hoping that the doctors would tell me the opposite that I didn't have a stroke and that I would be discharged soon to go home. But that was far from the truth; it was merely wishful thinking instead of accepting the medical evidence or the reality of my situation.

Medical evidence pointed to dysarthria (a condition in which the muscles used for making speech are weak or there is a difficulty in controlling them), which has slurred speech as its symptom. The agonising reality was I had to learn to talk in order to correct my slurred speech to start with. Moreover, I was placed onseveral medications on a daily basis to treat the stroke; overtime these medications began to have terrible side effects on me. I felt my body organs began to show signs of adverse effects of each fistful of pills that I dutifully swallowed every day.

With each passing day in the bed and taking doses of medications daily with attendant adverse effects, my courage, energy, confidence, passion, hope, self-esteem and strong-will began to fade away as apathy, self-doubt, despondency and lethargy settled in .I observed that when I was in denial of my medical situation because it was apparently unpleasant to me, my mind was affected and I became depressed and confused. I wanted to remain in bed all the time in the hospital; while I remained in bed, several questions were racing through my mind and I couldn't find answers to them.

Some of them are:

Why wouldn't they allow me to remain in bed?

Why did I need to get dressed and be ready to be seen by doctors?

Why did I need to brush my teeth?

Why did I need to eat my breakfast that early?

Why did I need so much medication and many regular checks in a day?

Why didn't they see how much pain and weakness my body is experiencing?

Why did I need to take many medications daily despite the many side effects?

Why was I always sleeping or feeling drowsy and sleepy in the daytime?

Why did I need to do physiotherapy every day?

Why was I in a wheelchair???

There were several questions that I found extremely difficulty to provide answers to truthfully in my mind.

Since I had been bed-bound for months without any form of exercise, my legs were numb; it seemed as if there was a heavy chain tied to them; they were swollen without sensation and I could not lift or move them .As my organs begun to suffer due to huge doses of medications, lack of physical exercise and others, my fluid intake was drastically reduced. So, I was put on a regiment of a limited amount of fluid every day; even if I was thirsty,I was not permitted to exceed the recommended daily fluid intake. For that reason, additional daily medication was prescribed. Thus, the regiment of medications and water intake per day had debilitating effects on my wellbeing.

Given my healthcare background, I knew the water regiment would have an adverse impact on my body as the body has no ability to store water for too long; it needs fresh water supplies every day and failure to take adequate water daily would result in dehydration.

Weakness or paralysis of any part of the body is very common after a stroke. From medical data, approximately nine people out of every ten survivors of stroke incident experience some type of limitations in muscle movement or inability for body muscles to move voluntarily. The two most common types of post-stroke paralysis are called hemiplegia and hemiparesis. Hemiplegia stroke refers to severe paralysis of one side of the body or paralysis on one vertical half of the body. On the other hand, hemiparesis stroke refers to a weakness on one side of the body, typically in the extremities like the hands. Hemiplegia may result in spasticity, stiffness and spasms in the muscles. Also, it may lead to atrophy, meaning the wasting away of the muscles. However, hemiparesis stroke is less severe than hemiplegia stroke. Hemiparesis stroke can make it extremely difficult for a victim to perform the basic daily tasks like grasping and releasing objects. In some cases, it causes loss of balance, increased difficulty in walking as well as muscle fatigue.

I experienced hemiparesis stroke given the extreme difficulty I suffered daily in grasping and releasing objects. At a point in the hospital, I could not hold a cup of tea: I had to be fed like a baby by the care assistants. Soon afterwards, I developed incontinence; because of my regular incontinence, I was placed in diapers and I felt uncomfortable wearing diapers daily. Incontinence refers to the lack of voluntary control or self-restraint over urination or defecation. Moreover, I noticed I developed panic attacks very regularly. Whenever I experienced panic attack, it often triggered episodes of incontinence and pain. Each time I had a panic attack, I would lack the ability to control my bowels resulting in passing out urine and waste at the same time with excruciating pain.

Urinary incontinence, known as the loss of bladder control was a common embarrassing and annoying problem that I had to grapple with for a period of time. This problem became severe as I often had a strong urge to suddenly urinate however I couldn't get to the bathroom in time due to my mobility problem. The incontinence occurs because of possible impairment of the muscles and nerves that assist the bladder to hold or release urine. On many occasions when I experienced incontinence, I would scream for help as I wouldn't want to urinate or defecate on my body; the frustrating part of the experience was it does not give me enough time to go to the bathroom. Sometimes, the incontinence occurred almost every five to ten minutes in small amounts with severe pain and discomfort, it always came when i had the panic attacks

Another challenging issue that developed in the early phase of hospitalisation was I suffered from hypnophobia, meaning the fear of falling asleep. Not minding the number of medications I was using daily, I just could not sleep adequately in the hospital. I remembered several nights that I refused to sleep in the hospital, even though I was tired and wanted sleep, but I was afraid to sleep. This situation might sound like irony as a sick person undergoing excruciating pain should be glad to sleep in the night so as to get some relief for a moment. From the health and wellness point of view, sleep is regarded as one of the greatest pleasures in life. Sleep in the night helps a person to feel rested each day. Sleep in the night is vital for a person as it protects against illness and facilitates quick healing from sickness.

In my case, I was afraid to sleep due to the fear that I might not wake up in the morning. So, I developed several techniques to keep me awake every night as I was afraid that I might die in my sleep. For example, I would leave my mouth open in the night to prevent me from sleeping. Also, I would sit on the edge of the bed all night thinking if I made myself inconvenient, I wouldn't sleep at all. Moreover, there were occasions I sat on the chair from night time until five in the morning to deny myself night sleep. At times, I would get back into bed after five in the morning time hoping that

Bolaji L Adebiyi

the movements in the hospital or the early morning hustle and bustle in the city near the hospital would not let me die. However, the habit of having a short sleep after five did not work well with the hospital system, as I was always sleeping when the doctors were conducting their ward rounds between nine and eleven am.

In spite of the fact that I possessed basic knowledge about some values of adequate night sleep concerning my health and wellness, the devil preoccupied my mind with the nasty, negative thought of dying in the sleep. Sometimes, the devil made me think that if I slept in the night and the sleep suddenly went from being awesome to a nightmare, and I couldn't wake up in the following morning that would be the end of my life. Initially, it didn't occur to me that my supposed survival strategies from death were inspired by the devil to further fight my recovery. After some time, the inadequate night sleep aggravated my high blood pressure.

Also, insufficient night sleep impaired my mental well-being and alertness during the daytime. Self-denial of night sleep heightened my depressive condition. More importantly, I realised very late that deficient night sleep slowed down my recovery process. Finally, the inadequate night

It is important to emphasise that the decision to withdraw my sleeping tablets created a terrible problem for me as I began to hallucinate in the night time. Hallucination refers to the experience of seeing things that do not really exist caused by illness or medicating. Hallucination is considered a sensory experience of seeing something that does not exist outside the mind, which is caused by different physical and mental disorders. When a sick person sees, hears, feels or smells something that does not exist, it is either the illness or the medication taken has affected the mind of the patient. Since I was on a regiment of medications, the administration

Rescued From The Claws Of Death

of sleeping pills was to bring about some orderliness in my mind during night sleep. Therefore, having personally upset the applecart through my devious sleep denial strategies, the payday came with a discomforting reality; the withdrawal of my sleeping pills resulted in a hallucination. In the midst of this unpleasant situation, hearing of strange noises continued unabated in the rehab and I couldn't sleep well. in fact, I heard strange voices sometimes directing me to jump out of the window of the hospital. There was an occasion in the night that I asked the voice, "How will I jump out of the window when all the windows of are locked?" I heard the reply of the voice audibly saying, "You can break the window with your head!" I give thanks to God as I reflect on this situation for not heeding the instruction of the voice. In my bad state of health, Jesus Christ did not leave me alone. In John 10:27-28, Jesus said, *My sheep hear my voice, and I know them, and they follow me: And I give unto them eternal life; and they shall never perish, neither shall any man pluck them out of my hand.* I believe my failure to heed the voice was not by my power, but by the grace of Jesus Christ, who protected me that I might have the second chance to make amend. He did not allow the devil to pluck me out of His hand so that I shall not perish. I give glory to God, Jehovah-Rapha, my healer.

It is important to emphasise that the God of Christianity is quite different from those of other religions where the creatures help their creators to fight a battle. In Christianity, no man or woman can help God to do anything; we cannot help our God to fight a battle or fight an affliction or fight an enemy. His almightiness or omnipotence requires no support system from a man.

> *15 Can a woman forget her sucking child, that she should not have compassion on the son of her womb? yea, they may forget, yet will I not forget thee.*

Bolaji L Adebiyi

> *[16] Behold, I have graven thee upon the palms of my hands; thy walls are continually before me.*

As a mother, I understood the huge import of the analogy that God made between Himself and a woman nursing a baby in the above verses. I knew the symbolism of the love of a mother for her sucking baby; I knew it was practically impossible for a nursing mother in her right mind to forget her sucking child. Whereas, the love of God for me is more than that of the love of a nursing mother for her sucking baby.

It must be emphasised that I had to contend with unappealing food items in the hospital; the food items served by the hospital for breakfast, lunch and dinner were well prepared, but they did not naturally appeal to me. Due to the constant pain in my body and what I considered the needless taking of my blood daily – oh yes, they took my blood everyday - I lost my appetite and felt frustrated. At a particular time, I stopped eating food. The moment lunch or dinner was approaching, it usually came with foul smell to me; the irritating smell was so much that I sometimes wondered how other people in the ward were able to consume the food served. Obviously the different meals were great, but I had no appetite for it. Consequently, I began to lose weight significantly. All efforts made by the doctors and nurses to make me eat were unsuccessful. The variety of foods that appealed to me were the Nigerian spicy meals, but the distance from my house to the hospital was some hours, which made it impossible for me to get regular meals from home or from friends. Each time some friends or family members or my pastors came to visit, they usually came with African meals or a set of meals for me. However, that opportunity only lasted for a short while as the medical team then placed me on a strict

12

Rescued From The Claws Of Death

diet regime. Thereafter, I completely stopped eating altogether because I just could not stand the hospital meals.

It was at this stage of starvation that I was told to take special shakes to enable me gain some weight. During this time, the consultants figured out that I would need surgery down the line as they said that my heart was functioning at less than fifteen percent. I received these special shakes three times daily since my body could not tolerate any other meals. Not too long afterwards, my strong aversion to the hospital meals led to another health crisis as it gradually developed into severe gastrointestinal issues and ulcer-related symptoms. A medical test conducted showed that my intestine appeared it had sores all over, and for me, warm milk was the remedy and what worked for me was to take warm milk regularly, hence the suggestion of shakes. Warm milk would provide a brief relief of ulcer pain since it coats the stomach lining; however, it could potentially stimulate the stomach to produce extra acid and digestive juices that might aggravate an ulcer condition.

Besides the gastrointestinal issues or ulcer, another critical health challenge I experienced was constipation. I never knew that I would or could sit on the toilet for about thirty minutes to an hour trying to pass waste. At one point in the hospital, acute constipation was the order of the day; at a stage, it grew worse to become chronic constipation with the consumption of more medications. Chronic constipation is a health condition that is usually characterized by difficult, tough, infrequent or incomplete excretion of bowel movements. Chronicconstipation involved straining, hard stools, and difficulty or inability to pass stools, which I assumed was caused by medications for pain, blood pressure and others. Chronic constipation persisted for weeks and it brought nasty side effects, such as excruciating pressure on and straining

Bolaji L Adebiyi

of the rectal area, development of tiny fissures around the renal area, faecal impaction resulting in acute abdominal pain, severe bloating, including vomiting, nausea and fatigue due to. Soon afterwards, I began to swell all over my face and every part of my body. My legs became swollen that I could not get in and out of bed by myself without the help and support of the nurses. This was an indication that some vital organs in my body were in trouble.

One day the medical team decided to conduct further medical tests to resolve acute constipation. After the test, the medical consultant came back to me and looked somewhat crestfallen. She told me that she was sorry that she had initially thought that they had blasted all the clots in my blood, but they had found many clots in my blood again. I did not fully understand the implications of more blood clots in my body as I was not in the right mood to appreciate the adverse effects of what she told me. However, the blood clots she described involves the possibility of the clots in my bloods and that the clot might travel to my heart and if they did, the incident could result to stopping the heart from pumping blood. If the heart ceased to pump blood, it would instantly lead to a heart attack. A friend with medical experience later told me that the clots in the blood could just stop the heart from beating any time from that moment. It was at this stage that I became afraid and all I wanted to do was to go home; I just wanted to leave the hospital and go home. I was sick and tired of being in the hospital for the first six months, so I began to discuss the possibility of being discharged from the hospital to go home because I was afraid of just passing away in the hospital.

During this time, anywhere I looked, i would see a snake anywhere and every where, which was quickly dismissed by the medical team as hallucination. Their dismissive attitude notwithstanding, I knew deep down my heart what it was. In

Rescued From The Claws Of Death

the hospital, I started seeing snakes in whatever direction I faced despite the fact that snakes are extremely rare to come by in Ireland as the weather of the country is unfriendly to them.

I thought I had developed ophidiophobia at this point: ophidiophobia refers to the fear of snake or fear of all things that are long and venomous. Whenever I looked at the tiniest line, itwould turn to a snake and I began to wonder if I was seeing live snakes. Out of curiosity, I would move towards the object on many occasions to examine if it was a real snake or not. Whenever I moved closer to assess the object, I would realize that it was a rope or just a line. As time goes on, I kept seeing snakes wherever I looked at any line in the hospital arena; by the special grace of God, I experienced a unique deliverance at a point when I felt I saw Jesus rising and smashing the serpent on the head.

I remembered the day we discussed my first discharge from the hospital, despite the fact that I was still on the wheelchair then. The ward manager had called my husband, my pastor's wife and I into his office saying that he did not know himself that a day like this would come when we would all sit together discussing my discharge from the hospital, he was happy for me that i get to be discharged home. However, i had a father, the Great Physician, Jesus Christ who does not work by a medical diagnosis. He often overwrites the medical verdict of death.

With the passage of time, the medical consultants recommended I should be referred to the rehabilitation centre . One of the reasons for the recommendation was to ensure I could resume psycho-motor activities. Normally, for a stroke patient to improve all fine motor skills after a stroke, the person needs to rewire the brain with some rehabilitation exercises. Moreover, the consultants believed the rehab centre would provide some great hand exercises to help improve fine

15

motor skills, including leg exercises, such as knee extension, hip rotation, ankle stretching and thigh squeezing. Soon afterwards, they prepared my referral letter to move me to a Rehabilitation hospital. Within a few days, my referral was effected and I was moved accordingly to the Rehab center.

3

My Experience At Rehab

I arrived at the rehabilitation centre toward the end of 2015. I was convinced within myself that the rehab was not the solution as I knew I needed medical attention more urgently than being at a rehab and the reason being that i was week and still struggling with pain in my stomach and legs. As I was settling down gradually to life at the rehab centre, another problem suddenly developed; I could not sleep at all as I was always hearing strange voices. During this time, I honestly wanted a good sleep, but I couldn't sleep due to disturbing noises from the environment.

It was an ironic situation as there was a time I devised strategies for not sleeping, but now I wanted to sleep badly and I couldn't sleep. The nurses were being careful to ensure I didn't have another fall to avoid further complications. If I needed to use the bathroom, the nurses or health care assistants would assist there; I was being thoroughly supported to walk to ensure total safety. There were times I saw other patients going

Bolaji L Adebiyi

home for the weekends, but I was not allowed for the reason that my case was critical. I was constantly been diagnosed by the medical team for one health issue or the other. Also, regular blood tests were carried out to find solutions to the incessant pain in my body and the constant use of medications; eventually, I became frustrated with the preventive restriction of my movement to prevent fall, the lack of improvement in my condition and I couldn't take it anymore.

I thought that the solution to my problem was not rehabilitation as I didn't have the energy to participate in any rehab activities.

I had a strong feeling that I developed a medical problem called aphasia while I was in the rehab centre. I observed at a time in the rehab that when ever the medical team or the nurses called at my bed during ward rounds about my condition, it would take me about two minutes to respond to any of their questions.

I also exhibited the same problem whenever my family members or friends came to visit me. When they asked me questions or exchanged pleasantries with me, my reaction time to process the information and respond was often delayed.

Aphasia is a form of impairment of language that usually affects the production or comprehension of speech, including the ability to read and process information, and write a response. Aphasia may occur due to injury to the brain most commonly resulting from a stroke in older people. Furthermore, brain injuries resulting in aphasia may potentially arise from head trauma, infections and others. From the medical perspective, aphasia can be quite severe as to make effective communication between a patient and doctors almost impossible. Moreover, aphasia can be mild or moderate depending on the level of its adverse effects on the patient.

Rescued From The Claws Of Death

In my case, I could categorise the degree of aphasia as moderate due to the fact that it adversely affected my ability to retrieve information such as the names of objects quickly: also impaired my ability to put words together to form coherent sentences or read information. I became a sort of embarrassment to the people around me and I felt terribly hurt inside when I noticed this condition. Consequently, I could not attend all the physiotherapy sessions organised for me; the physiotherapists and nurses concluded that i was not suitable for rehab as at that time and suggested I needed psychological treatment. I wouldn't blame them for making this conclusion because they saw there was no noticeable improvement in my condition, but it wasn't my desire to remain unresponsive to treatment.

There was a night that I could not sleep; I called my husband that he should come to the rehab centre. I was tired and infuriated for being at the centre and I wanted to come home. Also, l called my pastor and his wife to come to the rehab centre. When they came, they met my husband already seated but I was so angry with myself and my life that I just sat on the wheelchair and backed him. I refused to talk to him: he knew I was angry in my spirit. After intense persuasion that I should tell him why I wanted to see him, I told him and my pastors that I wanted to leave the rehab and that I was not happy here. I added that at a point in time I thought of calling a cab and escaping home from the rehab. They all agreed with my decision to leave rehab early. As they were discussing my referral back to the hospital with the management of the rehab center, I didn't understand for whatever reason, but I got a kidney infection again. By this time my feet were swollen and my stomach hurt so badly that I couldn't eat. Soon afterwards, I just could not stand it anymore because of the pain; I rolled and screamed on the floor until an ambulance was called to

Bolaji L Adebiyi

take me to another hospital. On getting to the emergency unit at the hospital, they found out that I had a very bad kidney infection. I received treatment for the same problem for about 10 days before I was later discharged back to the rehab center. And on returning to the rehab, the management of the rehab decided to discharge me back to the original hospital because I was not able to participate in the recovery plan and programmes they scheduled for me report stating that i was not a suitable for rehab because i need medical treatment more.

Returning to the mother hospital commenced treatment again for the second time, I was depressed, angry and frustrated with myself. Shortly after my feet were swollen, heavy, and I had no strength to lift them up into the bed by myself. It took me a great effort with the assistance of the nurses and care assistants to lift them unto the bed. After a few weeks in the hospital and communing with God at the chapel to supply me His grace for enablement, I began to do things on my own because I realized that doing so would encourage the medical team. I knew if the medical team noticed an improvement in my condition, they might start thinking about how to discharge me from the hospital. So, I started trying really hard with the help of the Holy Spirit to convince them that I was making progress toward recovery.

Fortunately for me, one of my friends told me that there was a chapel within the hospital ground where I could wheel myself to pray and meditate. I believed Jesus Christ must have directed the consultant to tell me to go to the chapel. So, I frequently went to the chapel to pray to God. I did not attend the Mass, but I would go to the chapel to pray when i twas quiet. One afternoon, I went to the chapel to commune with God; as Hannah did, I poured my heart to God intensely and passionately that I wanted to walk again.

Rescued From The Claws Of Death

As time when on after regular prayers at the chapel and I changed my attitude with the help of God, I began to make effort to do things on my own and the pain began to reduce. For example, I would go to use the bathroom on my own after I had been in the hospital for five months. I would go to the shop inawheelchair. I recalled going to the church in the hospital, filled out my name in a prayer form and made several prayer requests. One of my prayer requests was, "God, I want to walk again." It was a short prayer, but it was the embodiment of my desire at a time. Eventually, I started to do lots of physiotherapy in the hospital with a determination to go home by Christmas time by all means. I started walking with the stroller and later with the hand stick.

God answered my prayers concerning the deadline I set for Christmas: a few days to Christmas, I was discharged to go home temporarily for some days on the condition that I would come back every week for a check-up and blood tests. While I was at home, I still wasn't sleeping or eating well, but I had so much support from my immediate family, my pastors, family friends, and others. On one of those visits from Pastors and his family, my immediate family members were all in the bedroom chatting with me and trying to cheer me up. I didn't know what happened but I recalled that I suddenly heard my pastor's wife screaming my name and shaking me vigorously on the bed, as if she was trying to prevent me from fainting. I was informed later that my face suddenly changed again as if I was having another stroke, so an ambulance was promptly called and I was rushed to the nearest hospital.

I was taken to the Coronary Care Unit (CCU) of the closest hospital to me, where about five doctors attended to me; they tried to locate my veins to use them to give me some medications, but they couldn't. By this time my veins had all collapsed because I had been in the hospital for more

21

Bolaji L Adebiyi

seven months, where my was taken on a daily basis. The doctors tried to put needles in my body searching earnestly for my veins. When they couldn't locate the veins, they tried my groin and succeeded in administering the medications. Doctors were watching on me overnight. I did survive the night miraculously by the grace of Jesus Christ. I remembered the lead doctor for that night informed me two days later that "There must be a man from the above watching over you all night".I presume the doctor implied there must be a God in heaven who watched over me throughout that night. The medical team planned to commence dialysis at this stage, as I was not producing urine and I was swollen all over my body. Prior to the commencement of the dialysis, miraculously, I began to produce urine again as they had put the urine line in.

During this phase of my treatment, it was strongly confirmed that I needed a heart transplant which had a lot of requirements to fulfil in order to qualify for the surgery. A heart transplant or a cardiac transplant refers to a surgical transplant procedure that is performed on patients experiencing end-stage heart failure or suffering severe coronary artery disease due to the failure of other medical or surgical treatments. The heart transplant is a lifesaving surgical operation involving an extremely high-risk process. It required a very strong referral from a heart consultant with lots of letters, tests and evidence-based proofs. Given the severity of the heart condition, the medical team quickly organized the process as I was in a wheelchair and receiving intravenous infusions daily .Finally, after about ten days, I got the long-awaited bed in the CCU of the seventh hospital for further tests and assessments for the transplant.

All this while, my older brother Evangelist Kola Idowu (RI) had always told me that until I got to a situation whereby

Rescued From The Claws Of Death

I could talk to God by myself like a daughter talks to her father, I might not conquer the enemy of my life and be healed completely. He admonished me to stop asking others to pray for me: he encouraged me to remove my veil and go directly to Jesus and talk to Him. He stressed that I should bring my petitions, request and cry to God and reason with Him. He concluded that until I do all the above, I might just be going around in circles. Immediately after the admonition, I remembered the Word of God in Isaiah 1:18:

Come now, and let us reason together, saith the Lord: though your sins be as scarlet, they shall be as white as snow; though they be red like crimson, they shall be as wool.

When I internalised the above scripture, I recalled my spirit was emboldened and I took the admonition on board that I needed to take a bold step beyond the ordinary to reach onto my Father, Jesus Christ. I agreed with my brother that I needed to dialogue with Jesus more intensely about my situation. Also, I remembered the parable of the widow in Luke 18: 1-5 and the need to persistently petition Jesus Christ.

Following the spiritual insight obtained from these scriptures, I decided that I would not let Heaven rest as I would continue to knock on Heaven'sdoor until my Lord Jesus Christ answers me like the widow mentioned above. So, upon getting to the hospital for the seventh admission, I was determined to talk to God and bring my case file to Jesus Christ, the Author of my faith. The seventh admission to the hospital was a wake-up call for me: I wondered why I didn't feel that way for the past twelve months. I couldn't fathom why I failed to realise eleven months before now that I would probably die the way my mother died when I was just two years if I didn't knock the door of Heaven harder. I wondered why I forgot that I have a good father, the Great Advocate, who

Bolaji L Adebiyi

is ready and willing to plead my case before the "I am that I am". I didn't know why I forgot God does not want me to die before my time, but to live and declare the glory and praise of the Lord Jesus Christ in the land of the living.

I wondered why I thought that God was punishing me for my sin of disobedience to His Words or God was reprimanding me for being far from becoming a righteous or perfect woman. I asked my self some pertinent questions several times: "Is this the way God intended my life to end? Why did I get struck down with a terrible sickness when I wanted to accelerate the speed to fulfil my dream of obtaining a postgraduate degree and settling down to blissful family life? Is this the plan that God has for my life?" After asking these questions and many more, I thought about how an earthly father would not want his children, particularly his daughter, to suffer and be in terrible pain and discomfort that I had experienced over eleven months. I couldn't come to terms with why a loving God would allow me to go through this harrowing sickness.

Having got this realization, the Rhema of some scriptures above that I had read and memorised actually came alive in my mind. The Holy Spirit began to remind me of scriptures which lightened the burden in my heart. Brethren, it is important to read the Bible and dwell in the Word of God regularly, because there will come a time when you might not be able to hold the Bible, not to talk of reading it. However, whatever scriptures you read in the past and stored in your memory, the Holy Spirit would bring them into your remembrance in the days of adversity. The Bible says, *If thou faint in the day of adversity, thy strength is small* (Proverbs 24:10).

The only way to acquire strength before trouble comes is to study the Word of God daily by reading the Bible. Also, it's highly recommended to attend Christian fellowships,

Rescued From The Claws Of Death

seminars, conferences as well as read anointed books and tapes of true messengers of God. I could not have gotten the sheer amount of strength and courage that I personally put into this fight against the devil over my life without listening to the Word of God and learning from the Holy Scriptures prior to the days of adversity. During some fiercest spiritual battles when my pastors and husband were not around to pray with me in the hospital, I would quietly tap into my word bank or go to the chapel to have intimately intense conversations with God. When ever my Word bank activated my faith bank, it would catalyse my inner strength and power to keep me going. It is mandatory for children of God to equip themselves with the word of God. The amount of the word you have in your word bank is what will work for you in the days of adversity; during the trial of faith, you may not have the strength to search for scriptures in the Bible. The Holy Spirit will bring into remembrance the word of God in our hearts when you face a challenge from the enemies.

"But the Advocate, the Holy Spirit, whom the Father will send in my name, will teach you all things and will remind you of everything I have said to you." (John 14:26, NIV).

I remembered scriptures upon scriptures, such as, *"I knew you before I formed you in your mother's womb.Before you were born I set you apart and appointed you as my prophet to the nations"* (Jeremiah 1:5).I also recalled that even though earthly parents do forget their children, that God would never forget me.*But even if that were possible, I would not forget you!* (Isaiah 49:15).

Moreover, I remembered the story of Lazarus who was dead and Jesus waited behind until he was buried before He came and raised him from the deadso that the glory might be given to Jehovah and the world might know that Jesus could raise the dead. And I said to myself that I am not dead yet, I am still alive and breathing, so my case is better than that

Bolaji L Adebiyi

of Lazarus. The story of Lazarus in John 11-1-43 is a story of comfort and strength in the Lord Jesus Christ. As I dwelled on the story of Lazarus to strengthen my faith in the miraculous of Jesus, the Holy Spirit began to expound a new dimension of the story to me. The Holy Spirit made me to understand why Jesus could not be summoned at will to act as I wanted Him to deliver me quickly from the jaws of death.

It is important to acknowledge the involvement of helpers of destiny during our physical and spiritual helplessness, particularly when someone is on the hospital bed. I was informed that some brethren sent my name to their prayer groups and ministries praying for God's intervention in my case. Also, when the General Overseer of the Redeemed Christian Church of God, Pastor Enoch Adeboye, visited Ireland in 2016 for the Ireland Holy Ghost Service, I was in Coronary Care Unit (CCU) and could not attend the event, but he prayed on a handkerchief, which was sent to me in the hospital.

Despite the fact that I could not attend the event, my spirit was connected to it as I watched the entire programme online and I claimed all the healing prophecies and prayers declared on the pulpit by Pastor Adeboye and other pastors by faith that night. Several men and women of God visited and prayed with me in the hospital and at home; those that could not visit the hospital prayed over the phone from Nigeria, Ireland, the UK, the US and other countries.

One day, as I lay on the hospital bed and unable to move or sit up, I pressed the call bell to attract the attention of the nurses to assist me. I couldn't move my legs due to an intra-aortic balloon pump that was fitted to my body. The intra-aortic balloon pump therapy involves an invasive medical procedure, which helps the pumping action of the human

Rescued From The Claws Of Death

heart by using a tube that has a balloon at the end. It indirectly increases the cardiac out put by means of after load reduction. It works like a partner with heart assisting it is sharing the function of pumping of blood on a fifty-fifty basis. With the balloon pump fitted to my body, I was experiencing unusual pain as if something was pounding my body all over. At a time, I was very familiar with pain as I felt excruciating pains every day; I constantly put up a sad face daily because of the continuous pain in my body.

One day, I examined my life from childhood to the point when I was hospitalised, I realised that besides the fear of dying, I had been living in fear of losing my children too: the fear of losing my children might be connected to the trauma resulting from losing my first baby boy. I lost my first baby boy back in 2000 while in Nigeria and I detested the experience so much so that I prayed to God I didn't want to witness such saddening occurrence in my life again .Of course, all parents want to protect their children from harm or death as there is no reasonable mother who enjoys the experience of losing her child. Whether a child has great vitality or the child has a disability, keeping the child safe from harm or sudden death is always a top priority of a loving mother. Although, the simple fear sensation to protect my children from harm has been part of me, it has not developed into a phobia. I had experienced different fears such as the fear of the unknown, the fear of dying young like my mother, the fear of failing to make a meaningful mark in life and the fear of not reaching my full potential in life. I was conscious of the adverse effects of fear and I had been praying to God to take away fear from my life.

If there is any reader of this book that is susceptible to simple fear or extreme fear (phobia), I am believing God that our Lord Jesus, the Lion of Judah, will grant you the grace to overcome the spirit of fear. Rather than having constantfear,

27

Bolaji L Adebiyi

you will start working in faith in Jesus mighty name. The Scripture says in Revelation 12: 11:

And they overcame him by the blood of the Lamb, and by the word of their testimony; and they loved not their lives unto the death.

You will overcome the spirit of fear in your life from this hour in the mighty name of Jesus Christ. The Lion of Judah willgrant you the supernatural gift of courage to overcome the spirit of fear.

4

Divine Encounter

It is an unexpected happenstance that leaves a person with a fresh, unusual and deeper revelation of God's power, which makes a unique difference and leaves an everlasting experience. Some brethren who had personal encounters with the Lord Jesus Christ and the Holy Spirit in the past would agree with me that it is usually an unforgettable and memorable experience. Remember the story of Paul on his way to Damascus to persecute the followers of Jesus Christ. The scripture says in Act 9:1-9.

Paul had an unforgettable encounter with Jesus Christ which led to his outstanding performances in ministry for the rest of his life. The unique encounter Paul had with Jesus Christ spiritually,

In the course of my hospitalisation, I had begun to speak to God that I was not a sinner and that I had not killed or harmed anyone. I reminded God of how active I was with my family in His sanctuary and how dedicated we were as a

Bolaji L Adebiyi

family to the things of God. Also, I reminded him about my sacrificial offerings and giving towards the kingdom projects;I reminded God of how I had been a good girl and how I had loved and served Him. I was justifying myself to my maker. Curiously, I told God who said I was conceived in iniquity that I had no sin; I said to the righteous God that I was righteous. Funny enough, I was justifying myself to convince God that I deserved a better deal from Him than my current situation of interminable pain and dwindling vitality.

In twinkling of an eye, the Spirit of the Lord reminded me about the parable of Jesus Christ concerningthe men who went up to the temple to pray in Luke 18:10-14.

> *10Two men went up to the temple to pray, one a Pharisee and the other a tax collector.*

> *11The Pharisee stood by himself and prayed: 'God, I thank you that I am not like other people—robbers, evildoers, adulterers—or even like this tax collector.*

> *12I fast twice a week and give a tenth of all I get.*

> *13But the tax collector stood at a distance. He would not even look up to heaven, but beat his breast and said, 'God, have mercy on me, a sinner.*

> *14I tell you that this man, rather than the other, went home justified before God. For all those who exalt themselves will be humbled, and those who humble themselves will be exalted* (Luke 18:10-14, NIV).

As I was trying to justify my actions and righteousness before God while sitting beside my bed in the hospital, I

Rescued From The Claws Of Death

heard a voice instantly asking me some questions: Oh, are you righteous really? So, you think you are not a sinner? The voice added, "Let me remind you about your sins. The voice addressed all and in my foolishness i began to count my fingers arguing that my sins are not many, I further decicided to count them since i was too sure that they were not many. So i began to count my fingers, then the voice reminded me further saying that there was still more, so while lying there i counted my toes and my fingers until i losted counts. The voice, which I believed was the Holy Spirit speaking to me added, "Remember that I was on a bed where you could not move your legs and arms. I watched over you while you slept. I sustained your spirit when the doctors thought it was over with you. When the Devil wanted to strangulate you, I came to your rescue. When you couldn't pass out wastes, I kept an angel at your door day and night preventing the angel of death to come in to your room, people die here everyday but i kept you because its not your time yet . When the devil wanted to devour you, I snatched you from his jaw".

As I looked transfixed and speechless, the Psalm 130:3-4 flashed into my mind and it was dawned on me that I did not appreciate the love of my God.

> *3 If thou, Lord, shouldest mark iniquities, O Lord, who shall stand?*

> *4 But there is forgiveness with thee, that thou mayest be feared.*

When I realised my ingratitude, unrighteousness and thoughtlessness about the grace of God in my life and family, I wept profusely like a baby; I reflected on God's amazing grace, admitted my faults, confessed all my sins to Him and cried out to God for mercy. The moment I accepted the fact that I was a sinner, who needed the blood of Jesus to cleanse me, and asked God to accept me into the fold of His beloved, I noticed a great change immediately. Without doubt in my heart, this incident of repentance and humility before God brought peace and overwhelming joy of new birth into my heart. I felt the hug of God and the Holy Spirit; I developed unique confidence in God because i made peace with my maker. I observed my repentant spirit was a supernatural turning point that marked the beginning of my miraculous healing. Thereafter, I began to make vows to God that I would serve Him and testify of His goodness to the whole world. I told Him to give me a second chance to serve Him again and submit completely unto his will and directions for my life.

Moreover, my pastor regularly visited me on Sunday mornings to hold service with me; we would conduct the opening prayer, and worship, and had a brief sermon. I could recall a specific day my pastor and his wife came and they both began to worship and pray; the two pastors were moved by the Holy Spirit and they began to prophesy that "God, your daughter Lola would go all over the world to testify of your power and glory". And they would weep onto my feet like a baby. And for the first time throughout my sickness, the only people that I felt sorry for were my husband and children whenever I saw how concerned they looked. The next persons that I felt sorry for were my pastor and his wife. Being overwhelmed by the display of their love and concern for my healing, I suddenly found myself asking God to please answer their prayers as I saw how much pain they went through over the sickness.

There was a day my godmother and her prayer partner travelled all the way from their home town to the hospital where i was to pray for me .According to them, when they

Rescued From The Claws Of Death

got the bus station, they found that the last bus coming to the hospital for that day had left. As they were deliberating on taking a taxi to the hospital to see me, God sent them transportation to get to me that night. A bus came to pick just the two of them from their home town to where i was at no extra charge, They narated that the *Bus* pulled up and asked if they wanted to go to where i was They replied in affirmation. When they entered the bus they asked the driver why he came to pick them and the driver replied that he was given an instruction in the office that there were people stranded in the bus station that wanted transportation. Based on the fact that the bus came out of the normal bus schedule for the day, they believed God must have ordered the man, who instructed the bus station manager to advise the driver to come to pick them. Given the fact that they made it to the hospital that night was a miracle on its own: God divinely ordered their steps until they got to me that day. As they prayed, I felt the power of God fell upon me afresh.

The Holy Spirit began to teach me that the greatest way to show my gratitude is for me to share my testimony. The Holy Spirit ministered to me that it is payback time for the enemy. Initially, I didn't understand the import of "it is payback time for the enemy".The Holy Spirit broadened my understanding by explaining to me that the greated way to pay bach the enemy is for me to share my testimony. Furthermore that sharing this testimony of my amazing healing would be the greatest payback of all times when the devil has to take all the consequences of the adversity, pain, and suffering he inflicted on me in the past. The Holy Spirit said my testimony would decimate my enemies, the devil and his agents, and invariably makes my healing permanent. He added that if I wanted to avenge the enemy for all the pain and suffering that I went through, then I needed to share my testimony. He

33

Bolaji L Adebiyi

stated that as I continue to share my testimony and witness to God's unimaginable supernatural healing, then the miracle would continue to multiply in the body of Christ. According to Him, wherever I share the testimony of my healing with brethren and non-Christians, the faith of the believers shall be strengthened, while unbelievers shall receive Christ as their saviour.

Additionally, He said my testimony shall strengthen the faith of many believers undergoing a challenge in their lives in the supernatural intervention of God in their seemingly hopeless situations. Moreover, He stressed that my testimony shall inspire those on hospital beds, who have received the medical verdict of death, to trust in the Great Physician who reversed my medical death sentence, to reverse negative medical verdict passed on them. Also, God informed me that my testimony shall cause a rain of miracles falling on individuals who believe in the healing power of Jesus Christ. Finally, He said that those who hear my testimony and tap into it, shall ignite their faith in Jehovah Rapha and they shall receive their portion of the miraculous of the Holy Spirit. Therefore, I encourage believers and non-believers reading this book to have faith in the supernatural healing of God, trust in the Great Physician, Jesus Christ andthe Lord shall visit them with the strange act of His deliverance in the mighty name of Jesus.

I am trusting God that He would take my testimony beyond a situation where people read, listen or watch it and burst into tears in sympathy for me to a level of internalising the act of God in my divine healing to ignite their faith in the unending miraculous power of the Holy Ghost. They will come to the understanding that God wants to heal and bless his children every minute, every hour and everyday, if we have faith in His supernatural.

34

Rescued From The Claws Of Death

It is important to note that when God is working our miracle, it might not be apparent to the doctors and nurses, who often follow the rule books of medicine and healthcare, which are contrary to the golden rule book of God, the Holy Bible. Also, we should not be under an illusion that the Devil would take the defeat gentlemanly and work away in shame. The Devil is a nasty and incorrigible person, who could be annoyingly obstinate sometimes to accept humbling defeat that Jesus Christ often gives him until he causes Jesus Christ to give him a brutal knockout.

One particular day, after I had been in the hospital for almost twenty months, the consultants summoned my husband, my pastor's wife and I to a brief meeting; they said I was running out of time, and my body could no longer handle the number of medicines they recommended for my daily intake. Therefore, I was placed on a life support machine to help my heart function and to keep me alive until I could get a donor for the heart transplant. Prior to this period, the medical team had told me and my family that I needed a heart donor for a heart transplant. But while the hospital was searching to find a suitable heart donor that would fit into my special needs, my health grew worst. Some days later, some consultants had a brief meeting with me and my husband to explain the process of installing anintra-aortic balloon pump in my body. My husband and I were not enthusiastic about the idea of an intra-aortic balloon pump.

The WebMD, the American online publisher of news and information concerning human health and well-being, described an intra-aortic balloon pump (IABP), as a long, skinny balloon that controls the flow of blood through the largest blood vessel in the body called the aorta. The IABP device gets smaller when the heart pumps blood to enable if flow out to the rest of the body. The IABP device gets bigger

35

when the human heart relaxes so as to keep more blood in the heart.The doctor may recommend the installation of an IABP if the heart of a person isn't getting enough blood supply or it is not sending enough blood out to the rest of the body. This condition is referred to as cardiogenic shock, which may occurafter a heart attack when the heart is weak or due to potential heart problem such as *Arrhythmia* (i.e. when the heart doesn't beat in the regular rhythm), and *Myocarditis* (i.e. when an infection has inflamed the heart muscle).Also, an IABP might be used to help a patient recover from surgery in order to reopen or bypass a blocked artery near the heart.

The machine was surgically fixed in my body. A tube went into my body through my groin area, and I couldn't sit up at all: I always had to lie on my back. Naturally, I detested sleeping on my back in the hospital throughout the day and gazing endlessly at the ceiling. Initially, when the IABP was installed, I never knew that I would be able to sleep on my back for a day, not to talk of six months. It was inconvenient to maintain such posture for the day; the experience was gruelling because while sleeping on my back I brushed my mouth and drank water, ate food, urinated and defecated using various uncomfortably cold, bedpans every day. The discomfort experienced during this time made me eat less; also, constipation and vomiting became regular occurrences for me. Even though the bedpan was extremely uncomfortable, I would sometimes stay there for an hour to pass out waste, before i could go.

When the machine was first fixed to my groin arear, I was unhappy about the thought of having to lie down in one spot in the hospital not knowing the exact date I would have a heart transplant. There was no specific timeframe given by the doctors for me to get a heart transplant; heart transplant is a critical medical exercise with attendant protocol, and getting a

Rescued From The Claws Of Death

heart is not like going on line to order one, there is no specific timeframe to get a heart transplant, so I would have to hope in divine intervention to get one anytime. As a result of this realisation, I resigned to fate to bear the IABP in my body and lie down in the CCU until I get a suitable donor for the heart transplant.

While I had waited for the heart transplant and got stuck to the balloon pump machine for about nine monthts, my health deteriorated even further. At this stage, the medical team suggested the implantation of a left ventricular assistive device (LVAD) again just to save time. The medical team had offered this treatment option some months earlier and I declined it because of its possible complications. The left ventricular assist device (LVAD) consists of a pump that is usually implanted in some patients who have reached an acute end-stage heart failure. The LVAD is surgically implanted and it is a battery-operated, mechanical pump that has a capacity to assist the left ventricle (i.e. the major pumping chamber of the heart) to pump blood to all parts of the body. The LVADs may be used as a bridge-to-transplant therapy; when LVAD is used as a bridge-to-transplantation for patients, it supports heart failure patients who are extremely sick and waiting for donor's hearts to become available. AnLVAD is a life-saving therapy often used to enhance the lives of some patients that are awaiting a heart transplant. In this situation, a patient waiting for heart transplant uses the LVAD pending the time a heart becomes available. In some cases, the LVAD may help to restore a failing heart by preventing the need for an immediate heart transplant. Thus, the LVAD may assist the heart and other systems of the body to rest, heal or grow stronger prior to undertaking the stress of transplant surgery. On the average, some patients awaiting heart transplant may remain on an LVAD for a period of six to twelve months prior to the availability of heart transplantation. Usually, the LVAD affords many patients the opportunity to return home during the waiting time for a heart transplant with improved functional capacity for their hearts than they had experienced prior to the LVAD surgery to treat the case of congestive heart failure. Below is an image of a person wearing a left ventricular assistive device.

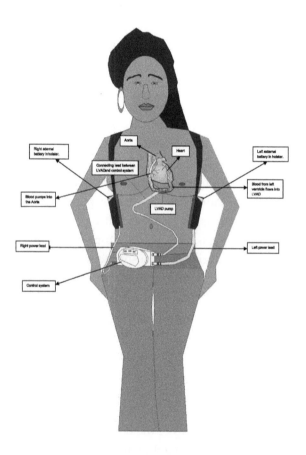

The medical consultants suggested that the LVADs should be administered to save me from dying. Assuming the

Rescued From The Claws Of Death

device was fastened to my body daily, I would have to charge its batteries every night in order for it to function during day time. If the device was strapped around my body daily, I would have to clean up the open wound in my body through which it would be fixed daily to avoid the risk of infection. And with all that done, I would have been taken off the waiting list for a heart transplant and not have been able to go through another surgery. Furthermore, the most horrifying aspect of this treatment is that the lifespan of the patientmight not last more than seven years or slightly more after the installation because of the high risk of infection.

After the meeting, my husband went home praying all night; he later called me in the morning and said he had sought the face of God all night and that all he received from God was the song below:

As my husband sang the song to me, I couldn't open my mouth to sing along with him; he advised that I should just meditate on the lyrics of the song and that God is a miracle working God. Prior to my illness, So, I began to meditate on the lyrics of the song that God is a miracle working God and that He is able to give me a miracle heart. I held onto to the miraculous healing power of God contained in the song.

A few days later, the professor of medicine, who suggested the installation of a left ventricular assistive device (LVAD) in my body earlier, came back again appealing to me to accept the alternative treatment as time was running out for me, but I declined the LVAD the second time. With faith in my heart, I told the professor that **I believed in miracle and that God was going to give me a new heart.** I added that the hospital would know that the new heart was mine because it would bear my name boldly written all over it when it arrives. The professor responded with a nod accepting the fact that it could indeed happen indeed.

39

Bolaji L Adebiyi

I remember my older brother, Evangelist John-Kola Idowu heard would always call me from the USA, he declared with authority and conviction in God that: "You, Lola Adebiyi, will not die before your time" He made the declaration bluntly and confidently in God having attended the Power Must Change Hands prayer programme held at the Prayer City of the Mountain of Fire and Miracles Ministries, Lagos, Nigeria twice on my behalf. I assumed he was spiritually charged as he must have encountered the outpouring of the Holy Ghost during the service .On one occasion, I was highly intrigued when I saw the team of pastors and brethren assembled praying and making prophetic declarations for me to be delievered from sickness, They decreed and prophesied that: that Lola Adebiyi shall live to declare the works of the Lord Jesus Christ in the land of the living."

Right from the time my husband had learned about the high risk associated with LVAD, here he rejected it by shaking his head in utter disagreement; he concluded that the LVAD was not the will of God for us, he assured and encourage me to wait on God for what he promised us, a new heart.

Following the decline of the LVAD, the medical team decided to commence palliative care because other organs in my body was failing I had begun to cry and scream for experiencing intense pain again. Palliative care is an end-of-life treatment, not only for a patient at the final hours or days of their lives, but more generally a health care designed for terminally ill patients that their conditions have become advanced, progressive, and incurable, to relieve the pain, anxiety, anguish, restlessness among others .At this stage of end-of-life care, I thought the Holy Spirit has mapped out deliverance for me as my faith unusually began to grow stronger than before. I began to trust the Lord more and more; I put my life entirely in His hand. As the medical team

Rescued From The Claws Of Death

continued to administer the palliative treatment every four hours, I couldn't eat because whatever I ate I would vomit almost immediately.

In spite of the fact that the Holy Spirit boosted my faith, human frailty in the face of daunting health crisis poses a momentary challenge to exercising my faith all the time. Human frailty refers to a condition of our existence when our beliefs about our toughness and ruggedness tend to draw on myth rather than on objective truth. It is a time of mental, moral and physical weaknesses resulting in a liability to yield to temptation. As time goes on with prolonged waiting for a heart transplant, I was tired, exhausted and fed up with life itself.

Proverbs 13:12 says, *Hope deferred maketh the heart sick: but when the desire cometh, it is a tree of life.*

Occasionally, frustration set in because I didn't know how long I would have to endure these symptoms before my desired change would arrive. But whenever I regained the consciousness of my father, the Lion of Judah, after drifting to hopelessness, I would ask God for forgiveness. Thereafter, I would put on the whole armour of God so that I can stand against the wiles of the devil (Ephesians 6:11) and prevent the Devil from stealing my faith in the awesomeness of God.

As the days passed by while I laid down on the hospital bed waiting for a solution, I grew closer to God than ever before as there was nothing else to distract me. I had no job to hustle to do; I had no need to look after my children; no events to attend and no academic study to bother about; so God had my undivided attention unlike when I was in good health sharing the time I supposed to give Him by attending to personal issues of life. I perceived I connected to God more, which is what God wants from all His children: God wants a quality relationship with His children, He wants to be able to talk to us and interact with us because He is a loving

41

Bolaji L Adebiyi

and kind God, not a wicked God. All He demands from every one of us is a quality, interactive relationship; God demands quality and regular communication with us, particularly if His call is upon our lives. He wants an intimate relationship with believers who are not specifically designated as apostles, evangelists, missionaries, pastors or prophets; as long as we believe in His son Jesus Christ as our Saviour, God wants to be close to us.

I must confess that when I was physically all right, I was easily distracted from maintaining an unbroken quality relationship with God; building a quality relationship with God requires investment in quality time. There were many different issues contending for my time and attention when I was in good health; my mind and brain were often preoccupied with job tasks, friends, busy with academic study, going to fellowship, caring for my family, including social life .On a daily basis, my time would be fragmented among all these issues In the course of investing quality time with God while on a hospital bed, I came to a full realisation that God wants to take His children far above having a beautiful family, a nice car, a cute house and other possessions. I discovered God wants us to fulfil our destiny, serve Him diligently and protect us from evil. Now that I really understand the purpose of God for my life, I have confidence in Him because I am convinced that I am actually living in Him. Based on this, I have decided to cling unto Him to enable me to fulfil destiny. A life without purpose is like a ship adrift without a rudder. It could take a decade for a person to identify his or her purpose in life, but once you have identified your purpose, you are then truly living.

I began to recall some scriptures from my mental Bible verse bank; by mental Bible verse bank, I mean the"Word Bank" where I stored Bible verses memorised from the past.

Rescued From The Claws Of Death

Remember that the Bible says that if we fail in the day of adversity, we fail because our strength is small (Proverbs 24:10). The strength of a believer might be small if he/she does not develop strength in the Word and faith in God; we need to study and meditate on the Word of God to build our Word bank.

The importance of having family and familia faces during sickness cannot be over emphasised, my senior sister Adetutu was with me for about four months in the CCU; she took excellent care of me by ministering the Word of faith to me regularly. Also, she relieved me of loneliness, isolation and despondency that had set in my life before her arrival. Regular communication and friendly discussion with my sister has some positive therapeutic effects on my wellbeing. My sister and I had opportunities to talk intimately, shared memorable stories, and laughed about funny events we recalled about our childhood.

Additionally, when the thought of my persistent health challenge overwhelmed us, we would cry intensely together. Frankly, I felt somewhat relieved daily with the presence of my sister as I was deeply connected to her. She would massage my swollen legs, and while doing so, she would prophesy and decree healing declarations that my legs would walk again and proclaim the gospel of the Lord Jesus Christ to the world. She told me from the very beginning that God said I was going to be okay and I held on to the word .But in a situation whereby I prayed and waited six months, twelve months, eighteen months, twenty-one months, looking for the divine intervention of God regarding my healing or heart transplant, brethren I must confess that sometimes my faith slacked due to the human frailties. When the time finally came for her to return to her family, I was not happy about the idea. I wished that she should be with me for longer because her presence

43

Bolaji L Adebiyi

and companion enhanced the quality of my life and healing tremendously to the extent that I forgot some of the adverse challenges confronting me in the hospital at that time. She was not happy leaving me behind either, but she had to leave to enable her to go back to her work and family.

I remembered the time my husband called to inform her that the doctors had given me two to three weeks to live. She made a video call to me and began to pray and cry, asking God why He had changed His promise concerning my health. She lamented that God informed her the day she heard I had a stroke that I would recover and walk again. She asked God repeatedly, "Why did you change your promise concerning Lola?"As she was crying during the video call I asked my sister in fear,"Why are you crying?" Moreover, I added, "Has God told you that I would not make it?"She replied that God has not told her that I would not make. I knew the faith of my sister diminished with the unfavourable news. I couldn't blame her because sometimes when some men and women of faith or their relatives are faced with some adverse, terminal health situations, their faith may relapse. Given the fact that God is a loving and kind sovereign God, He often forgives our unbelief.

A few days into the palliative care, I became very sick and could not eat or drink anymore. I was always in pain and cried profusely; on some occasions, I would scream and ask the nurses to call my husband and children. There was an occasion the medical team hospital rang my husband and phoned my husband asking him to come with my children to say their last goodbye as I might not make it till morning. On hearing the unpleasant message, he called our pastor and his wife, and they decided to come to the hospital immediately instead.

The truth is that they are the only persons that could

Rescued From The Claws Of Death

describe the battle that Jesus Christ fought on my behalf that night. All I could remember was I cried and told the nurses did I felt extremely cold. I was crying that i don't feel well, i was feeling cold and afraid, i knew i was in trouble. They check on me three to four times and concluded my condition seemed good and there was no drop in my temperature. In spite of their assurance about my temperature, I was extremely cold and could not stay still on the bed where some machines were fixed to my body. I felt my bed was vibrating due to my persistent shaking and crying. I continued to cry and asked the nurses to be seen by doctors because i knew things were not right. The nurses hurried out of my room to get the doctor but later returned in a few minutes the doctors were attending to an emergency elsewhere. I was really feeling cold, to the extent that I was shaking vigorously.

At one point, the nurses brought about eight blankets to cover me up to keep me warm. Despite this, I was still shaking with extreme cold and crying for help. She stated that they had checked my temperature, blood pressure and all the necessary health indicators were satisfactory. She added that the positive indicators showing I was all right made it absolutely unnecessary for any medication to be administered if there is no diagnosis.

However, when I continued to scream, cry and ask for help to ameliorate the nasty cold and searing pain, my pastor and his wife walked into the room; I noticed the expression of shock on their faces as they saw I was in an extremely agonising situation. I recalled they were pacing back and forth at the side of the room, praying in tongues and talking to the nurses about checking my vital signs again. During that time, my temperature had gone up to 40° and they quickly called for doctors. When the doctor came, all the medical

Bolaji L Adebiyi

team quickly put in another line for antibiotics because i had another infection from the lines for the ballon pump. Thant was the third time that my ballo pumb was changed from right groin to left and back to the right again as a result of infection. My body was so hot that I vomited up to two litres of all manner of materials from my stomach. The moment I vomited everything out of my system, (I call that deliverance) I felt amazingly relieve.

At that time, the doctors managed to put a line of the antibiotics that night and I slept off deeply till daybreak. In the morning, I woke up with fresh energy and feeling well, not knowing how I miraculously survived the night.

Beginning from the time I slept off in the night till the following morning, I noticed a positive, drastic, great change in my health and circumstance altogether. That same week, my recovery was accelerated unbelievably to the extent that everyone could not believe the speed of the recovery after the open heart surgery. The recovery speed was amazing. i was well known by the medical team by this time, because i had being leaving with them for almost ten monthts, every one rejoiced with me. the surgery that the medical professors had said that i might not get at 99.9%, that might be impossible for me to get a suitable heart even at ninety nine percent because that my immunity had dropped significantly and there was other complications with my kidney but Jesus Christ annulled their medical verdict.

Having crushed the head of the Devil by Jesus Christ that night, everything began to turn in my favour in rapid succession. It is only Jesus Christ that can do what no man can do. Suddenly, after the third attempt, a hundred percent match heart, the suitable heart came with my name conspicuously attached to it. This was a fulfilment of my prophetic declaration that I would get a new heart with my name written on it.

Brethren, please note that a closed mouth during the battle with affliction, will result in a closed destiny; we must use our mouth to make positive declarations about our healing because the Scripture says, *Death and life are in the power of the tongue: and they that love it shall eat the fruit thereof* (Proverbs 18:21).

I made the declaration in faith when there was no hope, i said afraid that I would get a heart. God did it for me and it became possible. Even before the surgery, some nurses and doctors began to congratulate me. There are a few healthcare professionals out there with huge faith in the divine healing of God. One day, one of the old nurses walked into my room and said, "Lola, you have paid your dues, you will get it and you will be okay", she stated unapologetically and with authority. This same nurse later told me after the surgery that God was not on holidays as you might have been thinking Lola. I believe God sent me so many angels in human form to assist in my battle against death. I give thanks and glory to God, Jesus Christ and the Holy Spirit for not abandoning me during my fight for life.

5

Prophecy Fulfilled-The New Life

One day, specifically a few months after my surgery, it was dawned on me that God has a master plan of escape in a time of adversity for my life and all of His children. He has seen from the beginning that at a point in time, I would need a new heart and God is the creator of mankind, He has spare parts of all human body organs in heaven in case a person needs a replacement due to any condition. Having experienced a gruelling affliction, prolonged hospitalisation and walked in the shadow of death, I appreciated the awesomeness of God more than ever before. I came to a full realisation that all the while God had me in mind and in His master plan despite the fact I was still lost in my own world doing things based on my own understanding.

I could remember ten years prior to my illness, when I had just completed my undergraduate degree programme, a colleague, who is a pastor did not have a car then to move around while my family had two cars. My husband and I

Rescued From The Claws Of Death

decided to bless him with one of the cars and I told him to come to our house to take the car any time he desired. The day he came to pick up the car at our home, he came with Pastor Francis Ola, who is a close friend of pastor. Pastor Ola had visited my parish several times in the past either to preach or carry out other specific church activities, and he still visits the parish till this day. On receiving these two men of God, I persuaded them to say a word of prayer as they were about to leave with the car. I don't be little the messengers of God; as these two pastors visited our home that day, I saw it as a privilege to have them pray for my family that morning. We prayed and after the prayer, Pastor Ola called me and my husband and told us that he saw a new life, a new baby in this home and that a new life was coming into our home. My husband and I thought that the prophecy indicated that we were going to have another baby. And ever since then I had been reminding God about His word through His messenger concerning the promise that a baby, a new life was going to come into my family. Year after year, I kept reminding God about the fulfilment of the prophecy; many times I asked God, "Where is the baby? Where is the new life?"I kept asking because I was confident that God cannot lie, and that every word He sends through His true messengers must come to fulfilment.

Furthermore, after my hospitalisation and I returned home, I still asked God, "Where is the baby and the new life that you promised me about 10 years ago?" I heard the voice of the Holy Spirit audibly and clearly saying: "Lola, it is you. You are the new baby and the new life that I was talking about". The Holy Spirit added,"Look at yourself, don't you see that you have become a new life? You have received the new life that I promised this family". With amusement, I said, "Whaooooo God, so you knew all the while that it

49

Bolaji L Adebiyi

was me that you prophesied about?"I added, "God you knew that I would need another life (heart) all along and you had organized a way of escape for me. You had a plan all along, you had a way of escape all mapped out for me while I didn't know since ten years ago, or from the beginning of my life". All the statements I could mutter are, "How mysterious are the ways of our God! How unsearchable and great is your wisdom oh Lord!"

The Things that I have Learned on this Journey

One great and unforgettable lesson I learned in the entire event is God specializes in accomplishing things that are impossible for men to do. When all human and medical efforts were exhausted, God arose for my sake because He wanted to take all the glory and praise for Himself alone. I cannot say it was a prophet, a pastor, a person or doctor that did it for me, I know without a doubt in my mind that it was God, Jehovah-Rapha, "The Lord Who Heals" (Exodus 15:26), who did it all and I return all the glory to Him. This is not to say I discountenance the role and support of all helpers of destiny that God used for my healing and deliverance, doctors etc, but the most gratifying message that I heard when I expressed my appreciation to them for their prayer support when I was in the hospital was they all confirmed that it was God who did my healing by Himself – it was God alone and God all the ways, not them. Hence, I attributed my deliverance to the grace of God, Jesus Christ and the Holy Spirit.

Another crucial lesson that I learned is that God can never be too late, even though He may delay but He will never be too late. If we reflect on the story of Lazarus in the Bible, Jesus intentionally waited two days after Lazarus had died to

Rescued From The Claws Of Death

glorify God and to demonstrate that He has power over death as a prelude to His resurrection. Although Lazarus' sisters complained to Jesus Christ that if only He had come early enough, their brother wouldn't have died, they failed to realise Jesus never comes up late to any situation. Jesus Christ, the master time manager; keeps time and appointment according to the divine agenda of His father, the El-Shaddai, who is the "God Almighty", in order to teach a great and unforgettable lesson. However, Jesus proved to Lazarus's sisters and the world that He never came too late; He is always on point and on time.

Note that all the battles and struggles that brethren are facing in life are not because of whom we have been in the past, but we face all these challenges in our lives because of whom we might become in the future. Which is why the Devil is fighting the children of God as he has seen our glory and the great place where God intends to take us in life. The Devil does not want us to fulfil the purpose of God in life. But, we give thanks to God as He had made an escape route for our success through His son, Jesus Christ by making Him the head over all things to trample down powers and principalities. In Ephesians 1:19-23 the Scripture declared our victory by stating:

> *19 And what is the exceeding greatness of his power to us-ward who believe, according to the working of his mighty power,*
>
> *20 Which he wrought in Christ, when he raised him from the <u>dead</u>, and set him at his own right hand in the heavenly places,*
>
> *21 Far above all principality, and power, and might, and dominion, and every name that is named, not only in this world, but also in that which is to come:*

Bolaji L Adebiyi

²² And hath put all things under his feet, and gave him to be the head over all things to the church,

²³ Which is his body, the fulness of him that filleth all in all.

Jesus Christ is set in authority over all powers and they have been made subject to Him. God has put all things under his feet; therefore all creatures, including the Devil and his host are in total subjection to the Lion of Judah. They must either surrender to Him in sincere obedience or fall under the pain of His sceptre and be subject to perpetual defeat and humiliation. God has made Jesus Christ the head over all things on the earth and in heaven.

Sometimes affliction is a learning curve that help to cleanse us, re-shape us and purify us as vessels of honour to God. In the course of the hospitalisation, I learned some unique lessons of life. I realised that I would not have made heaven if I had suddenly passed away during that ordeal, especially the morning I had the stroke. I would not have made heaven because I had so much garbage, anger and bitterness and unforgiveness hanging all over my heart. God saw all that and planed an escape route for me.

It was not a mistake on the part of my Saviour Jesus Christ to design another way of escape for me to work out my own salvation and stop all religious practices, but rather to seek for a real relationship with Him. God wants to establish a genuine and true relationship with us, not just superficial church attendance and activities. He desires a cordial, intimate, true and bonding relationship with His children to enable us to know His heart. It is easy to be the most active person in the church, yet heaven may not even see you or recognize you; please listen to me brother or sister in Christ, I am not condemning active participation in Church activities. They are rewarding and excellent, but we should move beyond Church activities to the realm of enacting a real intimacy and a cordial connection with God.

In Matthew 7:22-23, Jesus said:

> *22 Many will say to me in that day, Lord, Lord, have we not prophesied in thy name? and in thy name have cast out devils? and in thy name done many wonderful works?*
>
> *23 And then will I profess unto them, I never knew you: depart from me, ye that work iniquity.*

Brethren, don't get me wrong all the church activities are good and scriptural, but you would be a failure if all you do are mere religious activities without a personal relationship with the Lord Jesus Christ. I encourage you to endure all that you can as a true Christian soldier to build a genuine relationship with God in this world to make sure that you don't miss heaven, which is our final destination after the toil and trouble in this wicked, sinful world.

Furthermore, I perceive that God allowed me to go through all that I experienced during the entire period of the sickness to let me rediscover my purpose in life. Going by the things that He showed me and taught me on my sick bed, God took me through a spiritual rediscovery and reawakening. How he opened my spiritual eyes and mind and gave me a new direction in life which is more focused on serving and bonding with God rather than seeking personal gratifications in life. It would have been a disaster for me to have ended it all on the hospital bed without fulfilling God's plan and purpose for my life.

Bolaji L Adebiyi

For what shall it profit a man, if he shall gain the whole world, and lose his own soul? Mark 8:36 (KJV).

What is the use of material acquisitions in life if one does not make heaven? Whatever a Christian achieves in this world if he/she does not make heaven, all the achievements, riches, honours, academic laurels and others are vanities. For my twenty one months of hospitalisation, all i wore was pyjamas, meanwhile i has designer cloths, shoes and bags in my wardrobe but i could not use any of them, vanity upon vanity, all is vanity.

Permit me to say that if you are in Christ, whatever you are going through right now, God knows about it. It might seem like a mistake or an error, but God can turn that which looks like a mistake or an error to glory and blessing for you and me in order to exalt His name.Which is why He is God that does what pleases Him, not what necessarily pleases us. The fact that God converses with His messengers and children and uses mankind to accomplish some of His goals on the earth, He does not need the permission of mankind to act the way He pleases. For example, when I had a stroke in the church during my friend's wedding, I felt so embarrassed and ashamed of what had happened to me, but you need to see the rejoicing that filled heaven the day I went back to the same church where I suffered a stroke to stand on their altar to give all the praises and glory to God. I collapsed in the same church and could not walk and I was driven out of the place in an ambulance less than two years ago and I returned to the same place by driving myself and walking on my legs into the church to give Jesus Christ, the Great Physician, the glory and praise. Alleluia to Jesus Christ, the Balm of Gilead that cures and heals till today. He will heal and cure any areas of your life where you are going through a challenge in your health today in the mighty name of Jehovah.

54

Rescued From The Claws Of Death

"And we know that all things work together for good to them that love God, to them who are the called according to his *purpose."* Romans 8:28(KJV).

If you are in Christ, whatever you are going through right now, God knows about it. It might seem like a mistake or an error, but God can turn that which looks like a mistake or an error to glory and blessing for you and me in order to exalt His name.

Conclusion

In conclusion, I would like to say that prior to the adversity I experienced I did not fully understand the love of God the way I do right now. For God so love the world that He gave His best, His only Son over two thousand years ago for my life and the lives of other believers. I wish that I had settled down in the past to read the word of God more than now and understood who God really is. The fact is the devil does not really want Christians to know and understand who God is. The devil is afraid of this because once we know and understand who God is, and the ramification of His power, we will find it easy to approach Him confidently to deal a devastating blow on the devil.

For example, if I had a wealthy father and he promised me one million dollars, I would not doubt him because I know his financial net worth. I know that he has millions of dollars and what he promised to give me, he could conveniently afford it Naturally, I would not doubt his ability to fulfil his promise, the same thing with our heavenly father. If we take our time to study the word and know God more and understand how big and powerful He is, we would never doubt any of His promises to us anymore. There is nothing that we are going through right now that God does not know about. God does not only know about what we are going through, butHe has also designed a plan for our victory. The scripture says,

"No temptation has overtaken you except what is common to mankind. And God is faithful; he will not let you be tempted beyond what you can bear. But when you are tempted, he will also provide a way out so that you can endure it" (1 Corinthians 10:13).

God knows us so well and He understands our frailties that we can mess up at anything as we are not up to the standards of His power, strength and ability. As for me, God knew before now that I would need a spare part; He knew He would overhaul and renew my life before I could fulfil destiny in life. The Word of God states in Job 33: 22-25:

> *²² Yea, his soul draweth near unto the grave, and his life to the destroyers.*
>
> *²³ If there be a messenger with him, an interpreter, one among a thousand, to shew unto man his uprightness:*
>
> *²⁴ Then he is gracious unto him, and saith, Deliver him from going down to the pit: I have found a ransom.*
>
> *²⁵ His flesh shall be fresher than a child's: he shall return to the days of his youth.*

He knew all along that the claws of the devil would nearly tear me into pieces as he did to Job, but God knew what He would have an opportune time to deal a huge blow at the forehead of the devil. Just like the story of Jesus at the wedding in Cana when Mary approached Jesus that the guests were running out of wine, Jesus knew what He would do, but His time had not come. When His time came, He surprised everyone present at the event with a miracle that the world continues to narrate till He comes back. I am praying for you that you will not miss your time of deliverance,and you will not miss your season of a breakthrough in Jesus's mighty name. That issue of concern in your life that makes you shed tears in secret is not a mistake, it is not an accident, it is an indication that God had designed to launch your life to greatness. I will explain why I said so.

As I was leaving the hospital ground, I was leaving with a heavy burden in my heart to make the enemy regret ever messing around with me. I wanted to know why I walked through the valley of the shadow of death and I was poised to fight the devil and his agents dirty, but the Holy Spirit began to open up my mind into the word of God to see things from His perspective. He made me realise it is not by human power or might, but by the Spirit of the Lord that I overcame the devil. Thereafter, the Holy Spirit said to me that I am not fighting against flesh and blood but against principalities and powers. He told me that the only way to pay back the enemy for the evil and the pain that he caused me was to share my testimony. Furthermore, He told me that my renewed body was no longer mine, but it belongs to Him to use as He pleases and for His praise and glory. For the first time in my life, I got the total assurance that He was going to be with me all the way and that I had nothing to fear. He reminded me about the scripture:

"No one will be able to stand against you all the days of your life. As I was with Moses, so I will be with you; I will never leave you nor forsake you." ¬Joshua 1:5 (NIV).

Brethren, it is possible that someone called you trash, but God calls you a treasure. Do you understand how treasurable you are that He gave His only begotten Son for you and me, therefore don't trash that pain, don't waste it, but convert it to a precious ornament, a testimony to the glory of God. We are vessels of honour, sanctified, and meet for the master's use, and prepared unto every good work for the promotion of the kingdom of God.

Don't ever think of throwing in the towel. Remember that sickness, that pain, that sorrow, that accident, Jesus can turn them around in a miraculous way to give glory and praise to the name of Jehovah. Jesus Christ told me "I have to give you a second chance and my grace is sufficient for you", and I believe it.

God of the second chance granted Jonah the second opportunity to the people of Nineveh as He miraculously saved him in the belly of a large fish that swallowed him for three days and three nights. When Jonah showed remorse for his sin and surrendered himself to God, He commanded the fish to vomit Jonah out.

Jonah 2: 9-10 *But I will sacrifice unto thee with the voice of thanksgiving; I will pay that that I have vowed. Salvation is of the LORD. And the LORD spake unto the fish, and it vomited out Jonah upon the dry land.*

God was not done with Jonah yet; He commanded Jonah the second time to travel to Nineveh and prophesy to people of the city. Having learned the hard way, Jonah did not look back this time he immediately went straight to the city. The same way when I showed remorse for my sin and ingratitude to God, He granted me speedy recovery; also, He offered me the second chance like Jonah evangelised to the people of Nineveh, so I could evangelise to the world about His unending reckless love for my life.

Therefore, brethren when God says to that sickness or whatever is holding you down "let him or her go because he/she is my vessel", no powers in the hell can hold you down.

An example is when Jesus was going into Jerusalem and he requested for a donkey to ride to the city, remember the donkey was tied down somewhere. But at His commandment, they had to lose the donkey because the Master had a need to use it. May the Lord find a use for you in your Christian journey.

It was not me at all but the bigness of God that no power on earth can stand or deny. I am praying that what God did in my life He will do greater in your own life too from now on in the mighty name of Jesus Christ.

Paul's encounter with Jesus was the turning point in his life and ministry. He became zealous and passionate about Jesus Christ. The Bible says:

I have been crucified with Christ and I no longer live, but Christ lives in me. The life I now live in the body, I live by faith in the Son of God, who loved me and gave himself for me.(Galatians 2: 20, NIV).

The encounter I had with God during my travails in the hospital was a critical turning point in my life. The encounter was the driving force that propelled me to write this book to evangelise the awesome love, wonders and power of God, who snatched me from the jaws of death to remain a living soul to His glory. May the Lord Jesus Christ grant everyone reading this book a divine encounter to turn your life around miraculously for His glory forever in jesus mighty name i pray.

Amen.

Epilogue

What then shall we say
Rev 12: 11
'And they overcame him by the blood of the lamb, and by the word of their testimony, and they loved not their lives unto the death'.

The testimony here, is a practical application of the word of God in the face of death, coupled with victory accomplished for us through His death, burial and resurrection.***Heb 4: 12****'for the word of God is quick, and powerful, and sharper than any two-edged sword, piercing even to the dividing asunder of soul and spirit, and of the joints and marrow, and is a discerner of the thoughts and intents of the heart'.*

Rms 8: 31*What then shall we say to these things? If God is for us, who can be against us.*

The agony of Sister Lola's (the author) journey through the twenty-one months of hospitalization is a thrill of victory and the agony of defeating death delivered by practical application of faith in the word of God.For death could not hold Christ captive, we cannot be held captive by any form of death as well.

1Cor 15: 57*'But thanks be to God, who gives us the victory through our Lord Jesus Christ'*

Now Over to you

Having read this book, what do you desire?

Since God is not a respecter of persons, if He can give these kinds of miraculous healing encounter to the author, it means you are next for the miraculous. Victory over sickness, diseases, challenges of life and lot more.

Deut 10: 17-18 *'For the Lord your God is God of gods, and Lord of lords, a great God, a mighty, and a terrible, which regardeth not person, nor taketh reward'*

He doth execute the judgment of the fatherless and widow, and loveth the stranger, in giving him food and raiment' and all that is require of you is;

1. **To come unto Him.**

   Matthew 11: 28

   'Come unto me, all ye that labor and are heavy laden, and I will give you rest'.

2. **Accept and surrender all to Him.**

   John 1: 12 'for as many that received Him, to them gave he power to become the sons of God, even to them that believe on his name'.

3. **Learn of Him**

   Matthew 11: 29 'Take my yokeupon you and learn of me; for I am meek and lowly in heart; and ye shall find rest unto your souls'.

As you can see and have read in this epistle of testimony by sister Lola, Christ took away the burden of illness and break the yoke of sickness in her life. Same God is ever committed to your healing, deliverance, salvation and lot more. ***3 John vs 2*** *says, Beloved, I wish above all things that thou mayest prosper and be in health, even as thy soul prospereth.*

In a nut shell, I admonish you not only to read but also

key into the testimony contained therein for reproduction, for trust in the Lord that He is able. ***Eph 3: 20*** *'Now unto Him that is able to do exceedingly abundantly above all that we ask or think, according to the power that worketh in us'.* As you read this book, I pray that the mighty hand of God be mighty upon you, the blood of the everlasting covenant speak for you and speak against your adversaries, and the wonder working power of the Holy Spirit works wonder in you and your ministry.

Goodness Adebiyi
Maryland USA

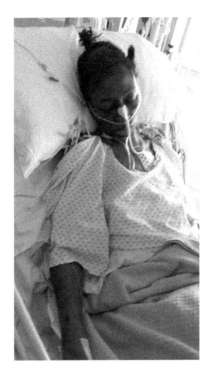
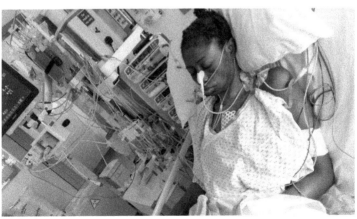

This is what I looked like during the hospitalisation.

Lightning Source UK Ltd.
Milton Keynes UK
UKHW020635230719
346664UK00005B/162/P